DINOSAURS AND THEIR DISCOVERERS™

The Dinosaur Footprints and Roland T. Bird

Brooke Hartzog

The Rosen Publishing Group's
PowerKids Press™
New York

Published in 1999 by The Rosen Publishing Group, Inc.
29 East 21st Street, New York, NY 10010

First Edition

Book Design: Danielle Primiceri

Photo Credits: pp. 5, 18 © Robert Reiff/FPG International; pp. 6, 22 © American Museum of Natural History; pp. 9, 17, 21 © Linda Hall Library; p. 10 © Roger Tidman/Corbis; p. 13 © Francesc Muntada/Corbis and 1997 Digital Vision Ltd.

Hartzog, Brooke.
    The dinosaur footprints and Roland T. Bird / by Brooke Hartzog.
        p.   cm.—(Dinosaurs and their discoverers)
    Summary: Describes the efforts of Roland Bird to investigate footprints left in various sites across the American Southwest by dinosaurs millions of years ago.
    ISBN 0-8239-5330-0
    1. Bird, Roland T. (Roland Thaxter), 1899– —Juvenile literature. 2. Paleontologists—United States—Biography—Juvenile literature. 3. Footprints, Fossil—Juvenile literature. [1. Bird, Roland T. (Roland Thaxter), 1899– . 2. Paleontologists. 3. Dinosaurs. 4. Footprints, Fossil.] I. Title. II. Series: Hartzog, Brooke. Dinosaurs and their discoverers
QE22.B538H37 1998
567.9'092—dc21   98-14720
                                                                          CIP
                                                                          AC

Manufactured in the United States of America

Contents

Fossil Footprints

We have learned everything we know about dinosaurs by studying **fossils** (FAH-sulz). When dinosaurs died, their bodies were covered with **sediment** (SEH-dih-ment). After many years the sediment became rock, and the remains of these creatures turned into fossils. These fossils help scientists learn about what dinosaurs were like.

But there are
some things
scientists
cannot learn
from fossils
that were
formed after a
dinosaur died.
Luckily, some fossils
were created by living
dinosaurs. Dinosaurs left footprints in mud or dirt. Over
millions of years, the footprints turned into stone. Fossilized
footprints are the only fossils left by living creatures.

*These are dinosaur tracks from a
sauropod found in Utah.*

Roland T. Bird's Discovery

Ever since he was a young boy, Roland T. Bird dreamed of becoming a famous dinosaur fossil hunter. He loved to ride around in the Arizona desert on his motorcycle. In the desert, Roland would imagine the days when dinosaurs had walked on that very land. One day, while Roland was in a **museum** (myoo-ZEE-um), he saw a piece of wood that had been **petrified** (PEH-trih-fyd). It was from a tree that grew during the time of the dinosaurs. He learned that he might find some of this wood in the Arizona desert. In 1932, Roland made a trip to the desert to look for petrified wood. He didn't find any petrified wood. But he did discover a dinosaur fossil!

Here Roland T. Bird is measuring a dinosaur jaw.

An Important Find

Roland took the fossil and sent it to his father. His father brought it to a museum. There he learned that the fossil was the jawbone of an ancient **amphibian** (am-FIH-bee-un). In fact, no one had ever known about this type of amphibian before. If the creature were alive, it would look something like a giant **salamander** (SA-luh-man-dur). Roland was proud of the fossil. When his father sent it back, Roland showed it to other people in town. One man who saw it told Roland something incredible. The man said there was a place nearby where dinosaurs had left footprints in the mud millions of years ago.

Over the years, fossilized footprints were found in other places such as New England.

Dinosaur Tracks

Roland found out where the dinosaur tracks were. He followed them for an entire afternoon and all the next day. The tracks were everywhere, and they were all different sizes. But they all had the same shape. Each footprint had three giant toes with claws on the end. The claws looked like they could be used for fighting and tearing meat apart. This made Roland think the tracks were made by **carnivores** (KAR-nih-vorz). He also noticed a few long marks. These marks looked as if they had been made by a tail dragging on the ground behind whatever had left the footprints.

Would you know that this mark is a giant footprint?

Dinosaur Water Fountain

The dinosaur tracks were on ground that was wavy. The ground looked like waves of water had run over the sand a long time before and had then frozen. Roland thought that dinosaurs might have come to this place to drink water. He also thought other hungry dinosaurs might have come there to hunt the dinosaurs that were drinking the water. While all of these dinosaurs were near the water, their feet sank into the wet mud around the ancient lake. After the mud dried up and millions of years had passed, the footprints turned to stone. The footprints became fossils. They helped Roland learn about the dinosaurs' **behavior** (bee-HAY-vyur) while they were alive.

Some of the tracks discovered by Mr. Bird were left by dinosaurs walking in muddy, shallow water. ▶

Learning to Dig

Roland began working for the American Museum of Natural History in New York City. He learned all the different **techniques** (tek-NEEKS) for collecting fossils. Roland learned to dig up fossils with tools, such as shovels and rock hammers. He used these tools to get the fossils out of the rock surrounding them. Roland then cleaned the fossils with small brushes. Next, he wrapped them up in **plaster** (PLA-stur). This was so that the **delicate** (DEH-lih-kit) fossils wouldn't break. He traveled all over the western United States collecting fossils that the museum could put in its Great Hall of Dinosaurs.

◄ *Roland traveled around the western United States collecting fossils for the museum.*

Strange Fossils

The museum sent Roland to New Mexico to bring back a huge plant fossil that a woman had found in her backyard. While he was there, the townspeople told him that he should go to see the fossils in Jack Hill's store. Some townspeople told Roland the fossils were footprints made by a man who was twelve feet tall. Other people believed the tracks were made by giant **Zuni** (ZOO-nee) Indians. Roland wasn't sure exactly what or who had made the tracks. He decided to go to Glen Rose, Texas, where the fossils were first found.

Roland Bird talked to many people and visited several sites to help him find out what had made the huge footprints found in Texas. ▶

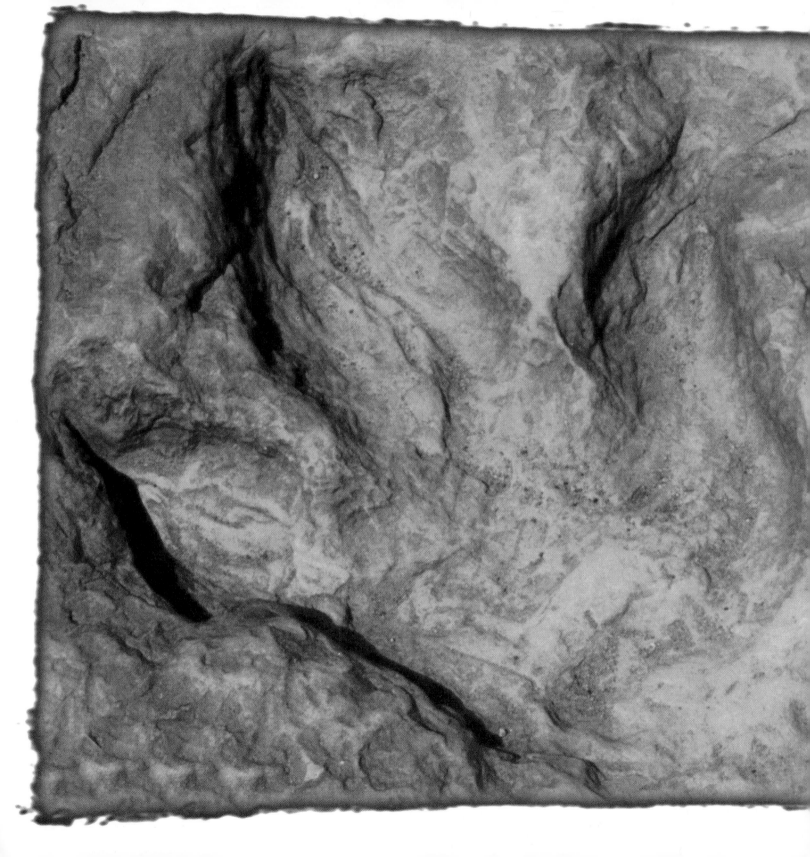

A Giant Footprint

Roland went to Glen Rose and talked to the people there. They told him about a place near a creek where he could find more dinosaur tracks. Roland went there and found many three-toed footprints. Roland also saw the marks dinosaurs had left when they walked through the mud long before his time. But he still couldn't **solve** (SAHLV) the puzzle of the giant human foot-shaped prints. Roland stood in the middle of a big hole, wondering what to do. As he looked around at the hole, he realized it wasn't really a hole. Roland was standing in the middle of the biggest dinosaur footprint he had ever seen!

Before Roland Bird discovered that the tracks were dinosaur footprints, some people thought that they were giant human footprints.

Dinosaur Giants

The giant footprint had been left by a **sauropod** (SOR-uh-pahd), one of the largest dinosaurs. Sauropod means "lizard-footed" in Latin. Sauropods include the **apatosaurus** (ah-PAT-oh-SOR-us) or **brachiosaurus** (brak-ee-oh-SOR-us). Roland found more giant footprints. Each was three feet wide. The prints were twelve feet apart. This meant each step these dinosaurs took was twelve feet long! Roland realized that the dinosaurs were the size of small buildings. He also saw that there were many footprints near each other. This fact told Roland that these dinosaurs probably moved around together in herds.

Many of the giant footprints that Bird found were made millions of years ago by sauropods, such as this one. ▶

An Important Discovery

People had known about giant footprints before Roland T. Bird. But they didn't know that dinosaurs had made the prints. People thought that the tracks were the footprints of giant bears or giant people that lived long ago. The scientists at the American Museum of Natural History were very happy about Roland's discovery. A huge piece of the footprint-filled rock that Roland found is still on display at the museum. It looks like a giant apatosaurus has just walked by and left footprints!

Web Sites:

You can learn more about dinosaurs at this Web site:
www.questionmark.com.au/qm_web/dino.html

Glossary

amphibian (am-FIH-bee-un) An animal that is able to live on both land and in water.

apatosaurus (ah-PAT-oh-SOR-us) A four-footed, plant-eating sauropod dinosaur. It was once known as a brontosaurus.

behavior (bee-HAY-vyur) How something acts.

brachiosaurus (brak-ee-oh-SOR-us) A four-footed, plant-eating sauropod dinosaur that had a long neck and tail and could be up to 130 feet in length and 40 feet tall.

carnivore (KAR-nih-vor) An animal that eats meat.

delicate (DEH-lih-kit) Easily broken or damaged.

fossil (FAH-sul) The remains of an animal or plant from the past found in the earth's crust.

museum (myoo-ZEE-um) A building where pieces of art or historical items are displayed.

petrify (PEH-trih-fy) When something, such as wood, turns to stone over many years.

plaster (PLA-stur) A soft mixture of lime, sand, and water that hardens as it dries.

salamander (SA-luh-man-dur) An amphibian that resembles a lizard but breathes through gills and doesn't have scaly skin.

sauropod (SOR-uh-pahd) Any of a group of the largest four-footed, plant-eating dinosaurs with long necks and tails and small heads.

sediment (SEH-dih-ment) Gravel, sand, silt, or mud that is carried by wind or water.

solve (SAHLV) To figure something out.

technique (tek-NEEK) A way of doing something.

Zuni (ZOO-nee) An American Indian people of western New Mexico.

Index